OVERCOME DEPRESSION

HOW TO BEAT DEPRESSION AND ANXIETY,
LEARN TO LOVE YOURSELF, AND LAUNCH
YOUR OWN HAPPINESS PROJECT

JONATHAN GREEN

DRAGON GOD BOOKS

Copyright © 2017-2018 by Dragon God, Inc.

All rights reserved.

Simultaneously published in United States of America, the UK, India, Germany, France, Italy, Canada, Japan, Spain, and Brazil.

All rights reserved. No part of this book may be reproduced in any form or by any other electronic or mechanical means – except in the case of brief quotations embedded in articles or reviews –without written permission from its author.

Overcome Depression has provided the most accurate information possible. Many of the techniques used in this book are from personal experiences. The author shall not be held liable for any damages resulting from use of this book.

Paperback ISBN-13: 978-1974268535

Paperback ISBN-10: 1974268535

Hardback ISBN: 978-1947667174

To Those Who Struggle in the Darkest Night...You Are No Longer Alone

CONTENTS

Don't Go it Alone	vii
Introduction	ix
A Note About Links	1
1. So Many Shrinks	2
2. The Freudian Method	7
3. The Approaching Cloud	14
4. Fighting the Demon	18
5. Emotions Are Thoughts	21
6. Control Your Thoughts	25
7. The Double Worry	31
8. No More Shame	41
9. It Takes a Village	45
10. Eternal Vigilance	53
11. The Emergency Happy List	57
12. The Future Looks so Bright I Gotta Wear Shades	61
More Information	64
Let's Soar Together	65
Found a Typo?	67
About the Author	69
Books by Jonathan Green	73
One Last Thing	75

DON'T GO IT ALONE

The hardest part of dealing with depression is going it alone. When you are in isolation, the night can seem so dark. Please join my FREE, private Facebook group filled with supportive people on the same path.

https://servenomaster.com/tribal

INTRODUCTION

I was six years old the first time I thought about committing suicide. I felt that my parents didn't give me enough attention and took me for granted; I didn't feel like I fit in my family the way that children on TV and the kids from school did. I felt distant from everyone, and I had a perfect plan. I would climb onto the roof of the house on Christmas morning before my parents woke up, and I would jump off. That would show them. I had this dream of getting revenge on my parents, and I imagined the look on their faces when they realized they didn't appreciate me enough, as they carted me off to my funeral. In my vision and in my imagination, of course, I was always there to watch everything, like an invisible ghost. Otherwise, what's the point?

As I grew older, I began to realize that I wouldn't actually be there – I wouldn't get to watch it, and smashing into the ground would probably really, really hurt. It took me a long time to discover that the force affecting me, this curse on my life had a name. Depression. It's an overwhelming force, and people who have never had it have no understanding of it. They think it's just sadness or perhaps just big sadness. If you are like me and you have dealt with this problem, you know it's much more, and it can become this monster of a problem you don't know how to deal with.

I never thought I would write a book about depression. I have recorded a few podcast episodes on the topic, and I have blogged about it, but it's not my main area. My followers are mostly entrepreneurs or people who want to succeed in building their businesses, but when you work alone, depression is more of a dangerous force because there is no one around. There is no one to check your depression or notice from the outside that something is going wrong. When you are alone, depression is a lot more sinister, and it can accomplish a lot more. You are already in isolation, which is depression's favorite way to start taking control.

I have decided to put together this book for these reasons. Whether you are working for yourself or not, you can join me on the journey of how I overcame depression and how you can accomplish the same thing.

A NOTE ABOUT LINKS

Throughout this book I mention other books, images, links, and additional content. All of that can be found at:

https://servenomaster.com/depression

You don't have to worry about trying to remember any other links or the names of anything mentioned in this book. Just enjoy the journey and focus on taking control of your destiny.

1

SO MANY SHRINKS

By the time I was eighteen, I had gone through five different shrinks, psychologists, counselors, and child specialists that I can remember. Maybe the number is even higher.

I started seeing my first psychologist when I was seven or eight. I don't have strong memories of my first psychologist, and I don't have a lot of memories of some of the ones in the middle. I just remember a few points throughout my journey, and I remember that I never really felt any different.

They would all try to fix me in various ways and with disparate techniques but nothing seemed to work for me, and once you have been to one or two shrinks you start to think the problem is unsolvable.

You start to think, "Oh my gosh, I'm incurable. There is no way to fix me; the problem is even bigger than I realized. Not only do I suffer, but I've also got the incurable form. I have the antibiotic-resistant form of depression, this monster that can be totally uncontrollable."

As I went through all these shrinks, I had a lot of these crazy experiences. All I really discovered was that my parents were paying people to talk to me and that these people were very easy to manipulate.

Every one of these psychologists, psychiatrists, and counselors has the same dream of having a case they can write a book about – a case so dramatic that it gets named after them. They want to be the psychologist that proves that split personalities or multiple personality disorder is real and not just an invention for movies.

For this reason, they are very open to suggestion, and as a child, part of my issue was that I wanted to please people.

I would begin to test the waters. I'm very aware of when I am talking to someone and they're bored. If I was talking to one of my counselors and I noticed that my stories were boring, I knew my problem wasn't that bad.

Objectively, my life was fine. My parents were wonderful; I was never abused, nothing bad happened. My family was extremely loving. The problem was my perception of reality, and not reality itself.

When I would talk about my life, there wasn't really any reason for me to be depressed, nothing major was happening. The problem was within me, and my stories were not very interesting to my counselor, so I began to make them more interesting.

I started making my stories a little more exciting, until it got to the point where what I was telling my psychiatrist had nothing to do with reality, and they were loving it. They would talk to my parents about breakthroughs and discovering these incredible depths within me. I would talk about the voices I was dealing with; I would talk about being afraid of my father, seeing a demon within him – all of these fantastical stories that weren't grounded in reality at all.

Finally, after my third or fourth psychologist failed to cure me, my mother came in for a joint session. I remember this moment quite vividly. I'm sitting there, telling stories to the psychiatrist of how I am so afraid of my father, and my mother looks at the shrink and goes, "Holy shit, you actually believe this? How stupid are you? Everything he said is a lie." I remember the look on the shrink's face – she was devastated.

Calamity ensued, she was unbelievably embarrassed that she had fallen for all of my stories. I said, "Look, I had to say something she wanted to hear. My normal life isn't interesting enough." I had been telling these fantastical stories and amazing adventures of a wild nightmare childhood, and none of it was true.

I was immediately thrown out and banned from the psychologist's office forever. She said, "I can't help you; I can't believe you didn't tell me your real problems."

Incurable

Looking back now, I understand exactly what happened. This particular psychologist, who was well-known and happened to be the trendiest and very expensive, was also very incompetent – at least in her dealings with me. She may have been able to help other children, but she didn't know what she was doing with me. She didn't understand my problem at all.

Along the way, doctors tried putting me on many different pills to make me happier and to control my mood, but none of my counselors or psychologists solved the problem. I would love to say that she was the last psychologist I worked with, but I had to go through one or two more after that.

Even after I was eighteen, my parents decided that I had a psychotic break and sent me to a psychologist to run an IQ test for my intelligence and an EQ test for my emotional problems, to figure out how I interacted with society. They wanted to see if I was a sociopath or something even worse.

They were sure something was wrong with me, so they sent me through for two full days of extensive testing (which I'm sure was very expensive, and even though we had a great health insurance, this was not a common experience). I was home from my freshman year at college when the results of all these fill-in-the-blank or multiple-choice tests came back.

It turned out I have a super high IQ, and I am slightly more aggressive than most people. I'm not bipolar, there were no psychotic breaks, and I had no psychological problems whatsoever.

By that point, I had taken control of my depression, so it was no longer a factor. My parents, just like many other parents, turned to modern medicine because they didn't understand their child.

Throughout this book, you may notice that I have the same feelings towards psychologists, psychiatrists, and counselors as I do about education. I am not a big fan of the way education is implemented in our society, and I'm not a huge fan of the way psychiatry works in our culture.

Reflection Questions

For the activities in this book, I can't recommend using a notebook enough. Just writing down your answers in your Depression Journal will be far more powerful than answering them in your mind.

1. Have you tried working with a counselor in the past? Write down your experience.
2. Was your first-time trip to a psychologist a good experience? Was it a bad experience? Did you enjoying listening to yourself and then trying to walk away believing that you felt a little bit better, even though you had to come back the following week for further treatment?
3. Did you feel like you were caught up in the treatment system or did it actually work for you? Did you have a positive experience?

Take the time to dig into your experience. This is your baseline, and it's a starting point for our progression through this book.

Activity

Stand in front of the mirror – or your cat or dog – for five minutes and talk about the main cause of your depression. Talk about trusting your biggest depression experiences and how they made you feel.

After five minutes, assess how your mood changes. Do you feel more depressed because now it's on your mind and you reminded yourself of certain aspects of your depression that you hadn't thought about in a long time? Or do you feel better because you talked about it and let the poison out?

This is a practical exercise to quickly assess which techniques work the best for you.

2

THE FREUDIAN METHOD

Psychology, psychiatry, or counseling is a soft science; it is not a hard science. Understanding the difference between the two is very important.

With a hard science, you can run an experiment and check the numbers at the end: the experiment either worked, or it didn't. You can mix together two chemicals and observe the reaction.

With a soft science, such as psychology or sociology, it's all based on opinions and feelings. The only way to tell if someone has been cured is if they say, "I feel like I have been cured." The only measurable effect is the placebo effect.

Most modern psychology is based on the Freudian method. Even though modern psychologists will say, "Oh no, I use a different method," it's going to be a derivative of the Freudian method no matter what they say.

The idea of this process is that you go to a psychologist, you talk about your problems, they decide how many times a week you have to see them, and in ten, fifteen or twenty years your problems begin to diminish.

We set out on these odysseys, and we spend these thousand or tens of thousands of dollars over our lifetime paying someone to listen to our problems. That is the part that everyone enjoys; there is something wonderful about having someone sit there, entirely focused on what you are going through. Who doesn't love a dedicated audience?

Everyone I know working in this field was at one point a patient. My experience of psychiatry is that it's a pyramid scheme. I had a friend who went through what I can only describe as an extreme psychotic break; he had to be sectioned for more than a month. This is when they put you in a facility (they have different names for them now, as you aren't allowed to call them an asylum anymore) to separate you from society until you feel better and ready to deal with the world. The people there helped him so much that he wanted to go into the same profession.

It becomes a cycle where the inmates end up running the asylum. I've always thought that these facilities were idyllic places where you would get to relax while everyone pays a lot of attention to you. That part of it I loved; I can understand wanting to disconnect from society, especially if you have an addiction problem or something else.

Give Away Your Power

This book is about dealing with depression specifically and how we approach that type of problem. The biggest issue with the Freudian method in modern psychology is that we are looking for someone to blame.

We all know that classic joke, "It's my mom's fault, everything wrong in my life is my mom's or my parents' fault." This begins the idea that you are not responsible for your destiny.

Every single piece of your life and every lesson that you learn that tells you that you are not in control of something weakens you – it diminishes you, and it takes away your power. If your mom is the reason you are depressed, then there is nothing you can do to fix it. If society is the reason you are depressed, there is no way to fix that either.

I've seen people declaring on the news or social media that politics is causing them problems. I even saw someone say that Twitter gave them PTSD (post-traumatic stress disorder). This shows that people don't really understand psychology, but what they want to do is give away as much of their power as possible and as quickly as they can.

I have friends who have dealt with real PTSD and seen horrible things in an actual war. PTSD used to be called "shell shock," and it came from seeing the shells and missiles blow up your friends. That is a different problem, and I do believe that it is something professionals can help you with.

I don't want you to think that I hate the whole psychological profession – I don't. I just believe that certain problems don't require twenty years to be dealt with. Throughout my own odyssey and my personal journey, it was only when I decided to take control of my destiny that the possibility of conquering my depression became a reality.

This modern approach to psychiatry is very much based on feeling good and not taking responsibility. It's very unusual for a psychologist to say, "Look, the reason your life stinks is because you are a bad person; you don't make good decisions, or you don't take responsibility."

When I was younger, I thought that I would love to help people – and I do love helping people – so I considered entering this profession myself. When I was having mental problems, I thought that the best way to deal with them would be by helping other people with theirs.

Then I realized that the business model is all about repeat visits. Once you get that patient with a sweet insurance plan, you'll want to get to see that person as many times in a month as that insurance plan will pay for. It's not about new customer acquisition, and it's not about fixing the problem; it's about treating the problem, and this is critical.

I'm a big fan of Neuro-Linguistic Programming (NLP). It's a different type of psychiatry, and it's a different way of dealing with your problems. NLP is all about letting you fix your problem and helping you overcome something in a single one-hour session, or over the course of four sessions within a month. And then you are fixed. That is something magical and powerful.

If you have to spend years fixing your problems, then I am not a believer in that. I don't want to think of life that way. If it really took twenty years, then I would still be suffering under a cloud of depression that maybe would finally start to diminish in two or three years' time.

Another drawback of psychology is that you sit in a room and all you talk about are the bad things in your life. "Let me tell you all of the reasons I am depressed," and the more you talk about something, the more you think about it, the more powerful it becomes.

This is the same reason I am not a big believer in marriage counseling. You are encouraged to list all the bad things about someone, and then you end up thinking about it more and more.

Often, in counseling sessions you'll say something that you forgot made you angry. That brings negative emotions back to the surface, and this is the part where you will see the that shrink's eyes light up with excitement. They'll say it's a breakthrough, but all you've done is dig up an old dark memory that you had forgotten.

You are spending most of your time empowering negative memories and digging up things that you have forgotten.

Not All Sunshine and Roses

I have had a lot of bad experiences in my life; I would not say that my life has been entirely blessed. Most of my bad experiences happened after I turned eighteen and after I conquered my depression, but I have certainly seen some darkness in my life.

I have lost some friends along the way, and I have nearly lost my own life a few times. I have dealt with addiction and other challenges throughout my formative years, and yet I don't want to talk about them all the time – I prefer to talk about happy things.

What we think about – our "thought life" – determines how we feel. It determines everything else that happens. If you have negative thoughts all the time, you will begin to have negative experiences; you will start to interpret the world through a negative light.

Two different people can listen to the same sentence but hear two completely different things depending on their current emotion. When you are in a bad mood, everything makes you mad. When you are in a good mood, you don't even notice the misinterpretation that can lead to madness.

Have you ever noticed that, when you are feeling depressed, someone can say something innocuous that you normally wouldn't care about, but now it really hurts your feelings because you are under the influence of a negative emotion?

The more time you spend talking about your depression, discussing it, drawing pictures of it, and making it real, the more power you give to it. That is something I don't like. I don't like to empower my depression.

If you go to your psychologist long enough, eventually you'll decide that your depression has sentience – it is a lurking monster that has eyes and a heart, a mind, and a plan. You will actively be at war with something that is as powerful as you, as if there were two masters inside your mind. You have been infected by an alien that is now trying to take control over you.

Grab the Bull by the Horns

When I was nearing the end of my high school years, I decided that I was sick of all those shrinks trying (and failing) to fix me. My parents had even gone to one who prescribed me "happy pills" without meeting me first. My parents told this quack what they didn't like about me, and he selected the perfect pill to fix me, sight unseen.

When you're a child, and your parents offer you a pill to fix you, it's a big deal. I remember thinking that I must stink as their child. Unfortunately, parents are doing this more and more. It's much easier to drug your child into compliance than to spend time connecting with them.

I tried these pills for a while, but they made me feel worse. They put a haze between me and my emotions and made me feel less human. I gave them a few months, and then I decided I wasn't going to take them anymore.

I made a decision to take control of my treatment. If there was a problem within me, it was my responsibility to grab the bull by the horns and conquer it. I would no longer depend on strangers to understand or fix me. I created this problem, and I would solve it on my own.

At the time, I was struggling in most areas of my life. I didn't have any friends. I felt lonely and an outsider most of the time, and my parents simply had no idea how to help me. This was the point in my life where I began to study and emulate a popular kid. I paid attention to how he acted and modified my behavior to match him.

That's how I faced my problem externally. I began to form tentative friendships, but they did nothing to help me when a crippling wave of depression would wash over me. I realized that I had to understand my enemy before I could defeat it.

Reflection Questions

1. When talking to other people about your problems, do your problems get bigger? When you talk to a psychologist or friend about your anger problems, do you feel your anger getting bigger or does letting out the poison make the problem go away for you?

2. When you're feeling depressed, how does it alter your perception of the universe? Do you feel more easily offended by the world around you? Do feel a little bit more sensitive – like your skin is a little thinner than usual? Write down exactly how depression affects you in your interactions and interpretations of other people's behavior.

Activity

It's time to take control of your destiny. Stand in front of the mirror, look yourself in the eye, and make a commitment. Promise to take responsibility for your struggles and your cure. It's time to become proactive.

You can take this one step further by writing down a mission statement and taping it above your mirror. "I'm in charge of my destiny." Or, "I will conquer my depression." Choose a wording that makes you feel empowered and inspired.

To go even further, make a vision board. Take a piece of poster board and attach pictures of what your life will be like without depression. Along the way, we will add more images to this vision board to inspire and strengthen your resolve.

3

THE APPROACHING CLOUD

Before we can overcome depression and face this demon, we need to understand the way the monster works. Depression has a very slow and sinister approach. Perhaps you have heard the story of putting the frog into hot water; it will jump right out, but if you put it in cold water and slowly warm it up, it will never jump out. Depression works in the same way; it comes in slowly like a cloud of fog, and you don't even notice that it's there.

I live on a tropical island right now; I live in paradise. Just the other day, I was outside watching this cloud come in. I turned to my wife and said, "I think it's going to rain soon," and it started raining immediately. I am able to predict the rain, but unfortunately only about five or ten seconds before it starts, rather than the twenty minutes that would be useful. By the time I notice it's going to rain, it's already too late, and we get soaked before we make it back to the house.

Depression starts off just like this cloud, slowly coming in. You begin to feel a little bit of a haze, and you think, "You know what, I don't feel like doing anything today. I don't feel like getting out of bed." Or, "I don't even feel like watching a movie; I don't feel like spending time with anyone today."

In this early phase, when depression starts creeping in, the first thing you experience is a desire to do nothing. You begin to isolate yourself from your friends, family, and coworkers. You create an island around you with the thought that you don't want to be around anyone else. "Uh, they just annoy me," and it is all negative.

We all have different ways we talk to ourselves inside our head, but the idea is to separate ourselves from the people around us. As we create a space or distance, depression slowly grows stronger. "I don't want to play a video game; I don't want to watch a movie; I don't want to go to a concert; I don't want to leave the house; I don't feel like making dinner. Maybe I'll order something later." We end up in a place where we don't desire to do anything, and that's where depression attacks.

Trapped in the Shade

Depression attacks our "desire center." That is where it slips in under the radar, and by the time you have realized what has happened, "Oh my gosh, I am feeling depressed," you look around, and no one's around. You don't feel like doing anything, and this cloud that was just at ankle level is suddenly above your head, and you can't see anything.

Most of us think of depression as the phase where the cloud has surrounded us; we don't think of the earlier stages. We only recognize depression when it feels like it has taken control and is an unstoppable force. This mindset is very limiting; we need to understand the process of depression, how it infects us, and how each person can have a slightly different experience. Depression might not feel like a cloud for everybody – sometimes it comes in a different way, but there are still warning signs and early phases.

Depression goes through a cycle: it starts small, it gets bigger and bigger, and then it peaks – it gets to a point where it is controlling you completely, until eventually you turn a corner, and depending upon how you suffer, that corner can sometimes be hours later. In my own experience, I would go through a six-week cycle of depression. I have been through both short and long cycles, but those are just my personal experiences.

Once you are inside the darkness, it is hard to escape. This sinister cloud is so effective because we don't take it seriously at first. We say, "Oh, it's just a little cloud of depression, it's no big deal. It's just around my feet; I can still see everything, I'm not worried about it." We become victims.

Even in my metaphors, depression is active; it's a cloud that's moving in. As you give depression more and more power, as you give it more action, you begin to become the victim or the receiver of that action. In order to break through depression, we are going to have to change a little bit of our mindset.

Fight in the First Phase

As I began to understand my depression, I realized that I had been waiting too long my entire life. I had always waited until the cloud was already there before I started to take action.

I realized that I had to act as soon as I noticed that the house was getting warm, rather than waiting until the rooms were filled with smoke. Depression and house fires are the same. The sooner you act, the better.

Waiting for the people around me to notice my depression would take far too long. The external effects don't show up until well into the peak cycle, when depression is at its strongest.

As you study your depression cycles, pay attention to the triggers and signs that a cycle is about to start.

Reflection Questions

1. How does depression affect you? Does it slowly creep up on you like a fog or does it strike you like a vampire when you're walking down the street at night? Most of the people I know experience a slow-build depression,

but each of us experiences depression in different ways.
2. Does your depression push you into a state of hibernation? Do you spend all day in bed and reject any overtures from friends or family? Is isolation a key component of your depression?
3. Have you noticed any new characteristics of your depression that you never noticed before? Does understanding these new components give you a new edge in your battle? Are you starting to feel hope again?

Activity

When you notice depression come upon you fast, or when it hits you suddenly, what is your trigger? Every time you have a fast-attack depression, write down in your Depression Journal the exact trigger and what caused your depression to flick. Was it talking to another person? Was it seeing something bad on the news? Has it started with a bad dream? That has happened to me.

As we work through this process, isolating your triggers and the causes of your depression will help us go further and further.

Activity Two

How do you visualize your depression? Do you think of your it as an active, powerful force, or as a passive force – something that is just an adjective like "tall" or "short?"

For this activity, draw a picture of how you see depression. It might be a picture of you as a knight, fighting a dragon. Perhaps your picture is someone setting a rainbow on fire. However you visualize or experience depression, take the time to draw it, so you have a clearer understanding of what you are competing with.

We are still developing your baseline, and the better you understand your depression, the more ground we can cover, and the more easily we can conquer this demon.

4

FIGHTING THE DEMON

Depression cannot be conquered passively. Someone else cannot defeat your depression for you; pills cannot make it disappear. The only way these things can be effective is if you remove all your emotions. If you take enough medication and you have no emotions at all, then yes, your depression will disappear, but so will your happiness and a significant portion of your humanity.

Before we get into the bigger part of the book – the part where I teach you how to conquer your depression – you have to make a decision. The decision is this: "I am going to defeat my depression." It's that simple. You are the actor, not me. I'm not going to conquer your depression; no one else is going to do it for you. You are in control, and you have to take the driver's seat.

Any time in life you give power to a third party – whether it's luck, fate, the universe, emotions, genetics, DNA, or whoever you want to blame – you throw away your power; you disempower yourself. This is why depression is such a big problem in our society.

Depression wasn't nearly so large of a problem fifty years ago. It is an adaptation of the elite; we have depression because we have enough time to be depressed. You don't starve from depression – you can still have an income, welfare or the dole, and support from your family.

A couple of hundred years ago, when there was no social net, and you said you were too depressed to work, well then you wouldn't eat. Either you would die, or you would find a way to break through your depression. Now that we all have the time to be debutants, more and more of us suffer from medical problems, and in fact, there are more diagnoses than there are people.

If you look at the top-ten psychological problems, there is enough for a hundred and fifty percent of the population to have a psychological problem. It is very unlikely that every single person in America is insane, and yet, if you look at prescriptions and treatments, that is exactly what the statistics tell us.

Too many people have this common problem that never used to be nearly as common. It is because of a shift in our culture towards disempowerment, victimizing, and blame.

Everyone is looking to blame someone else for their problems. This can be in your financial life or even your health. "I'm fat because the fast food restaurant makes unhealthy food." You could simply not eat there, but that would mean taking responsibility for your problems.

We are immersed in a culture where we don't take responsibility for our problems, but if we don't take responsibility for our problems, we don't have responsibility for our solutions.

Take a Stand

It is time to admit that you play a role in the depression that you suffer from. You have taken actions, or you've been passive in certain parts of your life, and that has allowed something else to fill in the gap; you have given up your power. Admitting that and making the decision to no longer be powerless will open up the floodgate to freedom.

Only when I stopped blaming the universe for my problems did things start to change. Taking responsibility for all your woes is scary, and admitting that depression is your fault is painful, but it's also empowering.

If you caused a problem, then you can fix it.

This step is not about making you feel bad; it's about giving you back the power in your life. It is about taking control. It's a painful step, but when you take it, the road to freedom becomes much shorter.

Reflection Questions

1. Have you spent most of your life blaming external factors for your depression? Were you blaming your parents, society, or the universe?
2. Have you noticed that mental problems are becoming more prevalent in our society? How is it possible that something that was once considered a problem is now something to flaunt and brag about? How many people on social media love to share their mental disorders?
3. Is it possible that all these signals are affecting you?

Activity

It's time for a second swing at this activity. If you skipped it before, it is now your chance to make up for that. If you already did this once, this will simply be an affirmation.

Stand up and take responsibility for your depression. Look in the mirror and commit to taking responsibility for your cure. Take control of your destiny, and you will be halfway to victory.

5

EMOTIONS ARE THOUGHTS

If you learn one thing from this book and forget everything else, please let this be the chapter you remember. Emotions are nothing more than a specific category of thoughts. Hopes, dreams, and memories – these are all thoughts as well, and yet we treat emotions like they are a special group.

This is a new invention of our culture; something we only started believing forty or fifty years ago. Before that, people thought of emotions in a different way. Once you realize that emotions are simply thoughts, they become absolutely and completely powerless.

Our society has empowered emotions by attaching additional language to them and treating them like they are a special category or under a protective glass. All thoughts are equal, but emotions are a little bit more equal than other thoughts.

We have this belief that emotions control us. Happiness controls me, therefore the emotion has the power, not me. The emotion, this part of my subconscious becomes the actor, the controller, and I am a puppet at the end of its strings. This is how most people view emotions and their thought life, but it is wrong.

You control your emotions. Allow me to demonstrate with a simple example:

You are lying in bed at the peak of your depression; you are in absolute and total malaise. You don't want to get out of bed; you haven't even turned on your phone, you let the battery die. You are disconnected from the world, and you are experiencing the most depressed moment of your entire life.

I want you to imagine that moment; imagine that feeling, and then you hear a beeping. You smell smoke, and you can feel heat – the fire alarm is going off. In that moment, every single depressing thought that you have will disappear.

Your body says, "Sorry, no more time for this, we have to survive." Adrenaline starts pumping, and depression is gone. Your survival instinct becomes everything you have to escape the house.

When you're outside, your depression will be gone because you will be so busy thinking about how glad you are to be alive. Your emotions completely reverse because you are in control of them.

Here's another example. You can't stop thinking about something; you have a list of chores you need to do today, but you decide to go to a movie first.

You get into the movie and are so distracted that you forget about the chores until the movie ends. You are able to push a thought aside while you are doing something else.

Emotional Two-Step

These are the two key components to this process:
1. Emotions are thoughts.
2. We can push thoughts to the side.

You can choose what to think about, and this is why I don't like any system that forces you to think about your depression, your negativity, and your problems all the time. The more you think about it, the more powerful it becomes.

The best way to shut down depression every time you see the thought coming is to say, "No, thanks!" That's how you block it. Imagine if you could reach out your hand to the universal stop symbol and push depression out of your life for good. In fact, this can apply to most emotions; we can proactively decide to be happy, or we can proactively decide to be sad.

I spent too long under the mistaken belief that emotions were in control. During my adolescence, more and more court cases pivoted on this idea. People were getting away with murder simply by blaming their emotions. "It's not my fault because the anger was in control."

This defense works because juries don't want to be responsible for their actions. We've created this powerful cycle, and every year a new ridiculous reason keeps someone out of prison. Just recently, a teenager was let off because he grew up "too rich." We are looking for any excuse to avoid responsibility for our actions.

Lawyers hold up emotions like mind-control aliens – as though your emotions can take control of your body and trap your mind in the back while they do their evil deeds.

Realizing that my emotions were just thoughts was a revelation for me. I began to feel more powerful in my journey to self-heal.

Reflection Questions

1. Do you ever feel like your emotions take control of your body? Do they become so overwhelming that you simply can't control yourself?
2. Have you ever felt so deep in the abyss that nothing could save you?
3. Do you think of emotions as something far more than thoughts? Are they outside your control?
4. How does thinking of emotions as thoughts and nothing more make you feel? Are you starting to feel empowered? Do your emotions feel so powerful that you're convinced I'm dead wrong?

Activity

Let's do a little exercise together. Pull out a mirror, or if you don't one handy, you can pull out your cell phone and put it on selfie mode to look at your face.

I want you to put on a big smile, a big toothy grin for two minutes. Count to one hundred and twenty, a full two minutes of smiling, and see how you feel. You will feel happier.

Immediately after, make a sad face for thirty seconds; you will feel your emotions changing. Your body can change your emotions because your physicality affects your emotions.

This is not a discovery or an invention by me; this is something that modern sciences have known about for a very long time. Emotions are controlled by your body, and they are nothing more than that. They are not special.

Activity Two

For the next few days, focus on your emotions and especially on moments of emotional shift. If you have a day where you are feeling sad, angry, or depressed, after writing down the trigger, do an activity that takes up of all of your attention.

Go to the movies, juggle, or play the guitar. Choose any activity that takes up a lot of your focus, give it a go and then see if you remember how you feel.

What you want to do is block the emotion and prove in a deep and meaningful way that emotions are just thoughts, and you have dominion over them. It is okay to focus on this activity for a week or two, until you are convinced and you fully understand how much power you have over emotions as a thought.

We want to learn to block each different emotion. Before we tackle just depression, let's lock in your power over your emotions in general. Block happiness, sadness, and any other emotion you feel coming in. Stretch your wings and demonstrate your dominance over your emotions.

6

CONTROL YOUR THOUGHTS

For many of us, finding out that emotions are just another form of thought and that we can affect our thoughts in a powerful way is a shocking revelation.

The first time I discovered this and began to experience it, my first thought was, "Why did nobody tell me? Why isn't this information out there?" If tough emotions can be dealt with very quickly and in dynamic ways, why is the information so buried?

Having experienced so many different points of the psychological spectrum, I realized that we live in a society that is obsessed with treating disease rather than curing it. The dream for a pharmaceutical company is for you to be sick enough to need their medicine, but not sick enough to die. That's how they make billions of dollars and are one of the largest industries in the world.

Psychology is the same thing. If you are going to a doctor for depression three times a week and you are paying a hundred dollars per session, which is mid to low range (some charge five hundred or a thousand dollars an hour), that person is making three hundred dollars off you a week. That's twelve hundred dollars a month; why would they want to get rid of that by curing your problem?

I am not saying that your psychologist specifically is a greedy mercenary, but the system as a whole is built around profit. Your psychologist is not there to help you; they are there to make money.

Helping you is part of the process, but see what happens if you ask for a free session. The help stops. Just like me, they are all capitalists. That is absolutely fine, but understanding the nature of someone's business is important before you do a deal with them.

Beliefs Control Thoughts

You have the ability to control your thoughts. Remember, if you are depressed and there is a fire, suddenly your depression disappears because you don't have time to think about it when your survival instincts kick in. You have more power than you think.

Depression works by tricking you into thinking that you have no power. If you believe that depression is sentient, it becomes a force on its own, caused by elements outside of your control. If you believe that depression is an entity that is actively working against you, you are giving away a great deal of your power.

The more of your power you give to depression, the less power you will have, until you get to a point where you've given it all away. This is where people start to make very poor decisions. Before you go too far down that path, begin to look at your depression as simply the result of bad thought patterns.

Our beliefs control our thoughts. Our thoughts control our decisions. Our decisions control our results. At a core level, your belief that depression is a powerful force makes it act like it is a powerful force. This is the frog in the boiling pot of water all over again.

Limiting Beliefs

I have a friend from when I was younger, from my college years. Probably one of the smartest people I have ever known and one of the most talented musicians I have ever met.

He grew up with very bad parents. His mother continually told him that he would never amount to anything and that he would never accomplish anything in life. This became his core belief.

Opportunities come to him all the time – more than a few people offered to pay for his college, help him start businesses or do projects with him. I, of course, tried to share with him some of the things that I do. But this core belief is too powerful. He believes that he can't succeed and therefore he doesn't.

It's like when you catch some crickets, put them in a jar, and then put the lid on top. The crickets keep jumping and bouncing to the top of it, but eventually they'll stop jumping that high.

You can take the lid off, and they will never jump out. Yes, that is a bit of backcountry wisdom, but it is still true. Once you are convinced that the wall is there, you'll stop touching it.

Learning the Wrong Lesson

When I was young, I watched a cartoon about testing who was smarter between a boy and a rat (of course it was a joke, it wasn't serious). They attached an electrode to the cheese and, after the first three shocks, the rat stopped touching it.

When they did the same with a cupcake, the boy kept touching it over and over again, getting shocked hundreds of times. The joke is that the boy doesn't learn, but maybe the cupcake isn't electrocuting him. Maybe what he is doing isn't as dumb as we think.

We get convinced that depression makes us powerless. We get convinced that depression can decide the course of our life and that certain things happen when we become depressed. Whether depression becomes more powerful depends upon you giving it power and isolating yourself.

You might start to think that when you're depressed your personality is terrible, "I don't want people to see me like this. I don't want them to suffer too. I don't want them to see how bad I am like this and never want to be friends with me again."

We almost hibernate; we curl up into our small cave of depression and we keep people out, because we assign too much power to this thought.

You have absolute dominion over your mind. In the previous chapter, I introduced an exercise you can do in the mirror. You can look up hundreds of studies, videos, and research all about how physiology and psychology are interrelated.

When you can change the way you hold your body language or add a smile to your face, it will affect how you feel inside. It is impossible to smile for more than two minutes and not have your mood go up.

If changing your face can make the sadness go away, how much more can a direct assault on the causes of your depression lead to the freedom that you deserve?

Reflection Questions

1. Are you still struggling with some limiting beliefs? Are you giving too much power to your emotions? Do you believe that your depression is different to everyone else's and therefore harder to tackle?
2. Do you want to spend the rest of your life paying through the nose to treat your problem or would you like to cure it?
3. Has depression been a part of your life for so long that the thought of losing it forever scares you? Are you worried that you'll start to miss those trips to the psychiatrist's office?
4. Are there any other limiting beliefs holding you back?

Activity

If we understand how our depression kicks off and learn to take control of our triggers, we can stop them and block the whole process.

For this activity, we are going to practice starting negative moods.

Stand in front of the mirror and talk about something that makes you angry – a bad experience or someone treating you poorly – until you feel that negative emotion taking control. When this happens, continue talking about those same things but make a smiley face until you reverse your mood to smiling.

I want you to try this back and forth for positive and negative emotions, over and over again. You can play this game of emotional ping-pong for hours.

When actors need to cry on screen, one method is to think about something that makes them extremely sad and have a trigger that can activate their tears. By the time we are eighteen or twenty, most of us have one of those experiences.

When I think about losing a best friend when I was seventeen, it is a very powerful emotional trigger for me. There is a particular song that reminds me of him every time I listen to it; I see his face in my eyes and I cry. It is a way for me to honor his memory because as long as I remember him, there is still a piece of him alive in this world, and so I carry a piece of Michael with me for when I want to experience sadness.

Sometimes you want to experience every emotion, because emotions are like colors on a painter's palette. Being able to use all of them is one of the beautiful experiences of this world. It is just important not to paint with too much blue or too much red. We don't want to only paint with anger or depression. We want them to be colors we use slightly.

Work on this activity and practice triggering different emotions. You can make yourself angry, sad, happy, or relaxed.

We're building upon an NLP technique called "anchoring." This is where we do an action that causes us to experience a specific emotion, and the first phase consists in locking in something that triggers this emotion.

We are going practice this activity a few times in order for you to understand how to trigger different emotions, but we don't need to trigger depression just yet. First, you want to master this activity and the process of finding positive emotions you can attach to a physical act.

For example, I have a joke that for some reason always makes me laugh even though it's not a good one. My friend Ollie told me this joke more than a decade ago. You are probably not going to laugh, and that's the point. It is my trigger, not yours. The joke is this: "What has two legs and bleeds?" The answer is: "Half a dog."

I'm laughing right now because it's my trigger for laughter. My friend wrote it when he was in Kindergarten, and he drew a picture of a dog; that's why it's so funny. There is a ninety-nine percent chance that you don't think that joke is funny at all, but that's the point. You have to find your own trigger.

Our first-level triggering is having a particular joke or a story that raises or lowers your mood. Then you can attach a physical action to permanently embed the emotion in your physicality. If I pinch my right earlobe every time I tell that dog joke, eventually, I will start laughing anytime I pinch my earlobe.

We can remove the intermediary step. I can touch my pinky to my thumb every time I hear that song to trigger my sadness. This is true anchoring, where we have a physical act that we tie to a memory or emotion.

I have used this technique many times in the past. When I wanted to stop feeling bad about my weight, I sought an activity or an action that I could perform. I would use my anchor every time I felt fat, and the feeling disappeared. It was a negative trigger. With more advanced NLP, you can create a trigger to stop your depression, but it's far easier to just start a happiness cycle.

Anchoring is a powerful NLP technique that has worked very well for me in the past.

7

THE DOUBLE WORRY

I grew up a very paranoid child. When it came to disasters, I was very creative. It was like having a *Final Destination* movie living inside my head.

I could always envision thousands of ways for me to die every day and I grew up thinking about that all the time – all the different disasters that could happen, everything that could go wrong.

When you combine intelligence, free time, and creativity, you have the perfect blend to live in a perpetual state of fear. I was afraid of everything that could happen, and all these fears turned me into a double worrier.

A double worrier is someone who worries about worrying. I dated a girl in my late twenties who was an excellent double worrier, far better than me. She was always worried that she was worried too much, which caused her to worry more. She would get caught up in these unbelievable worry cycles.

I read a study in high school (this is one of the revolutionary, key moments of my life) saying that ten percent of the things you worry about might happen; they are within the realm of possibility. Ninety percent of the things we worry about never happen. Ninety percent.

This turned me into a reverse worrier – like what you want to become. If you are worrying about something, that means it probably won't happen. This is the reverse, the mirror image, or the black swan effect.

The black swan effect is that unexpected things will happen; reverse worrying is that unexpected things happened in your past, but the things we expect and prepare for won't happen.

Terrible Predictors

Casinos invest considerable amounts of money in security; they put cameras everywhere and always watch for people who cheat, to make sure that money doesn't leave the floor if it was won unfairly. That is the primary area where casinos invest their money. Of course, they also spend a lot on vaults, security, and other elements, but their core focus is on the floor of the casino.

A good cheat who is really brave and living on the edge might steal a million dollars if they are cheating the casino on the floor. That is nothing when they are inside a building that cost a billion dollars – it's one-tenth of a percent of the cost of just building the casino in the first place.

The ten biggest losses in the history of Las Vegas had nothing to do with cheating. The biggest one was a tiger disaster. A tiger attacked one of the two performers, even though they had both done thousands of shows with these tigers.

There are a couple of pieces to this story that most people don't know, as they just read the headline. The casinos had extensive insurance against the tigers going into the audience; they were prepared for that.

Whatever happened if a tiger got into the audience, the casino would not have lost any money. It would have been horrible, and many people could have been hurt, but it would not have been a financial disaster. They had cover for that, so everyone's medical bills would have been paid.

People who would no longer be able to work would be covered

for life. Everyone in the audience had a layer of protection over them because the casino foresaw the possibility of this disaster.

What the casino managers didn't foresee was the possibility of the tigers attacking the trainers who had worked with them for twenty-five years. One of the trainers was hurt, and the casino lost a great deal of money – tens of millions of dollars, maybe even more – in medical bills, in promises in the contract to the performer, and in lost revenue from unperformed shows. The performer obviously couldn't work anymore, but fortunately, he has lived and recovered since then.

Here's the part of the story that most people don't remember: the performer saw the tiger going for the crowd and ran in the way. He realized something was wrong, and he threw himself in front of the tiger.

Whether or not you like tiger tamers, you have to respect someone who does that. I have a great deal of respect for someone who stands in front of danger like that to save a group of strangers.

From the casino's perspective, him jumping in front of the tiger was the worst thing that could have happened. His one act of bravery nullified all of their preparations for the future. They were right in their prediction that a tiger wouldn't attack a performer.

What they didn't think of is that if the performer saw the tiger about to attack the crowd, he would throw himself in the way. Because they didn't predict that, they lost a huge amount of money. What they worried about and thus prepared for didn't make a difference.

We worry about things that will never happen.

When I discovered that for every ten things I worry about, nine of those will never happen, worrying became the ultimate freedom. One simple revelation turned my anxiety into the source of my freedom. Changing one belief altered my thought life.

All the different ways that I thought I might die or suffer a calamity became my shield. I realized that I could never predict what would go wrong next.

My inability to predict the future meant that each time I thought of a new calamity, it was virtually guaranteed never to occur. Twenty years later, this single belief still drives a great deal of my happiness.

Activity

Let's test your predictive ability together. Write down the ten worst things that ever happened to you in your life. I know that it is an intense moment, but this activity is very important because it will break one of the chains between you and depression.

Write down the ten worst things that have ever happened to you and next to each one, answer this question with yes or no: did you ever worry about this happening before it happened?

This is a powerful activity, spend some time with it. Looking at the worst disasters in my life, none of them I had ever even considered being worth worrying about. I can tell you some of them.

My Worst Predictions

1. When I was eighteen, my friend died in a horrible car accident because he wasn't wearing his seatbelt. I had never even considered it. I am a paranoid seatbelt wearer, and I was even before this happened, but that really pushed me over the edge. I became obsessed with seat belts in college, and I'm still very obsessed with car safety because of what happened to my friend. I wasn't in the car with him at the time, but I do know he was someone who didn't wear a seatbelt. He drove like a lot of teenagers do – thinking they are invulnerable. That was one of the worst moments in my life.
2. When I got to my graduation ceremony after university, there was an asterisk next to my name saying I wasn't supposed to be graduating. There was a glitch in one of my courses. They had tried to call me, but because I was

graduating I moved to a new house, so I didn't get any of their messages, and I didn't find out until graduation day. Probably one of the worst days of my life, and I had no idea that was coming. I had to spend two months doing some extra credit work for two teachers. They changed two dumb grades, and I still graduated a year early. I just didn't walk across the stage.

3. A few weeks ago, my wife and I lost a child. She was pregnant for six weeks and had a miscarriage. It's a horrible experience, and we were not prepared for it. I recently acquired a great medical insurance, and it took me a lot of research to find a good medical program for my family. It doesn't cover pregnancy issues until after the first year, so we waited a few months for her to get pregnant in order to be covered by the insurance. We didn't think about the possibility that she would have a ton of medical problems in the first six weeks of her pregnancy.

These are the three worst things that have happened to me. As always, I lead from the front; they are not things I love talking about, but you deserve to know what I have experienced to really see that this activity is powerful. The things that we worry about rarely happen.

Activity Two

After you finish predicting the past, there is a second activity that will be very helpful for you. Write down ten things you are most worried about happening at the moment.

As you build this list of worries that are in your mind, realize that there is a ninety percent chance they won't happen. Statistically, none of them will happen. When we try to predict even small things, they never come true.

On television, they are constantly offering predictions about what the weather will be like in ten, fifty, or even a hundred years. Every single day, people are talking about global warming from both sides of the argument, and believe in it or not, I don't care.

Here's the thing. The weatherman still can't accurately tell me if it's going to rain tomorrow. We are terrible at predicting the future. If we can't predict the rain, how can we predict an ice age? That's a question to think about for a moment.

Let's look at that in a bit of a more practical way. Let's dial it in from looking at the world, and we'll try to bring it to something in your life. We can't even predict small conversations.

When I was younger, I used to write down an outline for when I would try to call a girl and ask her on a date. I would prepare for everything, writing down big branching trees made of, "I'm going to ask this question, and she'll say yes or no." Or, "I'm going to do this, and either this or that will happen."

I'd write down twenty layers, and I would have a whole plan, an entire flow chart, topics to talk about, how to work my way to ask her out on the date, to get everything perfect so we could have the perfect conversation.

Every single time, I got to thirty seconds, and I would rip the sheet in half; the conversation had gone nothing like I predicted.

One time, I called a girl, and her boyfriend answered. That was a surprise – I thought she was single. She certainly didn't tell me that she had a boyfriend when she gave me her number.

I've also had the brother answer, and I've had the father answer. All of these have happened to me. I've called, and a girl said, "Oh, I thought you wouldn't remember my phone number." That one was fun. I've called, and the girl was in the car; I've called, and the girl was in the hospital for an emergency – she's hurt, and I could not have called at a worse time.

After a while, I realized that planning for conversations is a waste of time. I can't even predict ten seconds into the future; I can't prepare for it. All of the things I prepared for didn't happen. Once the girl's father answered, I came up with a plan for when he would answer again. I had a plan for when a brother would answer and one for when a boyfriend would answer. It was never the same person, so then there was a plan for when a girlfriend or a cousin would answer. It was always someone different, so I'd end up with bigger and bigger sheets, but it did not matter because the bad things from the past did not repeat themselves.

Very rarely has something bad repeated itself in my life. The one thing that happened to me twice is I got ditched at both proms. Junior year, the girl left me at the prom. Senior year, the girl really took advantage of my prom.

The second girl didn't realize she picked someone who had spent a year thinking about what he would do if he got a chance to talk to the girl the year before, so the second time, instead of me leaving in tears, the girl left in tears.

Time is Precious

We have thoughts that lead nowhere, and time is your most valuable resource. The time you spend worrying about stuff is wasted. You are not a good worrier, and neither am I. The things you worry about will probably never happen.

Every time you worry about something, realize that means it's probably never going to happen. You can now look at that list of ten things you just wrote and recognize that none of them is ever going to happen.

Regaining all that thought-time that I used to spend worrying was amazing. I stopped feeling so busy. I started to have more time to think about and do the things that I actually enjoy.

For far too long, my worries about the future would trigger depression cycles. Realizing that these worries were just thoughts allowed me to push them to the side. They weren't visions of the future; they were just annoying insects buzzing around my brain.

Reflection Questions

1. Do you look at the future with hope or trepidation? Or do

all the talking heads on the news leave you shivering in your bed at night? Are you worried about the coming apocalypse?
2. Are you a double worrier?
3. How does learning that most of the things you worry about will never happen make you feel? Are you starting to see the light at the end of the tunnel?
4. Do you have limiting beliefs about the future and your ability to predict it? Are you using decision-calculus math to justify your worry on the basis that a small percent chance of something terrible is still worth worrying about?
5. Does worrying about the future affect whether or not your bad prediction will come true?

Activity Three

We are going to continue to build upon our anchoring from the previous lesson. Our activities are cumulative, and we're moving forward with some really inspiring progress. There are two things you're going to do for this activity.

1. Every time you worry that something bad is going to happen, write it down on your Depression Journal. We are going to track your statistics over the next couple of weeks and then we are going to use an activity similar to what card counters do in Vegas.

Every time you worry about something bad happening and then it happens, you add one point to your score; every time you are wrong, you take away a point.

Write down each of the things you think is going to happen and then track whether it happens or not. At the end of every week or at the end of the month, however long you can dedicate to this activity, add up your score. The longer you do the activity, the lower your score should be.

I want you to see how bad you are at predicting the future. You are the equivalent of a Las Vegas a cooler. A cooler's job in a casino is to stand next to someone who is lucky and affect them. Whether or not you believe in luck, this is a real job, and there is even a movie about it.

If you predict something bad will happen, I'll bet against you every single time. I will gladly put money on it. If I just bet a dollar on the first time you predict something, I have a ninety percent chance of winning back and making another dollar, and then I just reinvest and take my two dollars and bet against you again to double it. Now I've got four. Do it again; now I have eight. If I stick with you for a month, I'm a millionaire.

Betting against your ability to predict the future is the surest bet I can make. There is a ninety percent chance that you will be wrong every single time. I like them odds.

2. The second part of this activity is to use your anchoring from the previous lesson to break your worries. It is okay to worry about something for a moment with a fleeting thought.

If you worry about a boat catching on fire (I'm standing next to a boat right now, so that crossed my mind) it's pretty unlikely, since it just rained significantly out here. It's fine for a fleeting thought like that to pass through, even when it's clearly ridiculous.

If you start to feel that worry gaining strength or a foothold, or if you think about it for more than ten seconds, then that worry starts to be a thought. What I want you to do is to use one of your emotional anchors to break it.

I want you to try a few different things to get a feel for the power of your emotional palette. Breaking it with happiness, joy, or laughter is very powerful, but you can even break it with sadness. Obviously, you will then end up feeling sad, but the technique still works.

Worry is just another emotion, and I want you to see that you can break any emotion with any other emotion. Anchoring just makes this process easier.

Instead of having to go and watch *The Notebook* to be sad, you can pull your physical trigger – stick your finger in your ear, touch two fingers together, make a specific hand gesture, or slap yourself on the hip. Use whichever physical anchor you created. When you reenact that anchor, you can capture the desired emotion quickly and break the worry in half.

The purpose of anchoring is to be quick with triggering your emotions so that you don't have to do something that takes a long time. Most of the triggers that I have developed over time are quite short.

As soon as I hear the first few seconds of a sad song, or as soon as I hear that short, hilarious dog joke, my emotions shift. Just pronouncing those last two sentences, I went from really sad to really happy. That is how powerfully and quickly you can shift emotionally.

8

NO MORE SHAME

Admitting that you have depression carries a self-inflicted stigma with it. I don't look down on anyone who suffers from depression, and I don't know anyone who does. Normally, when you admit you have depression, you think you are admitting something far worse.

One of the things our society has been doing lately is changing the names of a lot of diseases. When I was a child, we had shell shock; now we have PTSD. We had manic depressive; now we have bipolar.

I think bipolar sounds worse. They change the names of these diseases so that we, as a society, can change our associations with them. The problem with that is it can make mental illness confusing.

Sometimes people tell me they suffer from something and they mention a new name, but I don't know what it means anymore. It took me a long time to figure out that bipolar and manic depressive meant the same thing.

When I was younger, I had some friends who were manic depressive, and I understood that; they had high energy and then low energy, they were happy and then sad. That made sense to me. When they called it bipolar, I thought that meant they had two different personalities, which sounds far worse to me.

When we tell people we have depression, we think they are going to look at us like we are insane. We are worried they won't know what it means. Depression hasn't changed its name in a long time, but a lot of the definitions of the diseases have been altered, and sometimes the change is subtle.

Autism became autism spectrum disorder; they widened the definition and added two more words after it, but autism spectrum disorder includes a wide variety of things that we previously didn't think of as autism. If you are my age and you learned that autism was much wider, it really affects your perception.

It's very stressful to think about telling all of your friends, "I'm insane." It feels like you are saying to your friends and family, "Hey, I can go crazy at any moment and come at you with a knife."

We are afraid and think this is what they are going to hear when we talk to them about depression: "I need to be in an asylum," or, "I have a massive mental defect." But we don't – all we have is a small problem with thought control.

Remember that depression is also about isolation. Shame is a great way to create isolation. During those first phases, when the fog starts coming in, depression keeps you from telling anyone.

In the next chapter, we are going to discuss tactics to break depression and make it almost completely powerless – it's taking the teeth right out of the tiger.

Everyone in my life knows about my depression; it's not something I hide. I wrote this book because I was talking to one of my super fans and I asked, "What should I write about next? What would be a valuable book for you?"

He asked me to write a book on depression because he liked the information I shared about it in two or three podcast videos. He found it helpful, and because I like to give people what they want, I am working on this project in response to that.

When I was younger, I used to listen to the song Dear Shame, which talks about shame almost like it was a dirty paparazzi reporter.

Shame would go through your garbage looking for your secrets; shame would look for ways to blackmail and control you. That's what shame is. When we personify shame, it makes sense: shame is a blackmailer with no power.

When we have secrets, people can use them against us; when we don't have secrets, shame becomes powerless. When someone tries to blackmail you, and you say, "You know what? I'll take those photos and post them online myself," the blackmailer loses all of their power and enter a state of absolute terror because they have tried to blackmail someone who can't be blackmailed.

They have started a war they have no ability to win. If you take depression away from your closet, if you take it away from the area of secrecy, it becomes far less powerful.

We have these ideas about how people perceive us, but they are wrong. Most people don't care. If you tell someone that you suffer from depression, they find it almost as uninteresting as hearing you talk about a dream.

We all have reasons why we are nervous about sharing our issues. When I was younger, my parents were very uncomfortable with my mental issues. They thought the mental problem was far bigger than it was, and their worry fed into my worry.

I didn't realize something was wrong with me until I realized they were worried. Their worry fed into mine and it became a more powerful force. As parents, we can affect our children negatively with our worry. It's hard to know what to do, and it's hard to say "don't worry" when you are a parent, but when your children detect it, they become more worried.

Reflection Questions

1. Do you consider your depression a secret shame? How does the thought of telling the people in your life about your depression make you feel?

2. Can you see how breaking through that stigma makes your shame powerless?
3. Has your depression used shame as a tool to control and isolate you?

Activity

Write down the reason you are afraid of talking about your depression and the way depression gets a hold of you. It's different for everyone.

Maybe you are afraid that other people will describe you as having a mental problem, or as being dumb. Maybe you are afraid it can cause a problem in your career. There are certain careers where it can cause a problem – for instance, if you are a police officer, a fireman, or a soldier.

In some professions, if you say that you have any kind of mental issue, it can negatively affect your career, and that is unfortunate. But we are going to adapt to that, and if there are certain people in your life you can't tell, that's okay.

Maybe you have a specific experience – one of your parents said something, or you heard someone say something, or maybe you are in a relationship with someone who hates people who have depression.

Oftentimes, when you ask them, you will find out that they had an experience in their past, so they pass along this chain. They dated someone who had depression; now they hate her/him, so they hate all people with depression, and you are afraid of saying anything. You're trapped, and you feel like you can't talk.

Whatever your fears are, I want you to write down why you are afraid of people finding out.

9
IT TAKES A VILLAGE

Depression is a silent killer. It is a ninja, and a ninja depends entirely on secrecy and surprise attacks. If you flash on the lights and everyone points their flashlights directly into the ninja's face, the ninja will lose every time.

Ninjas never win at face-to-face; they always kill you from behind, they poison you, they sneak in – that's how they work. If you ring the alarm bell as soon as you see a ninja coming towards your castle, it's game over for that ninja – that ninja will be running away.

Ninjas only have two modes of attack: sneak attack or running away. They never stand and fight, they never form a line or phalanx, and there's never a military unit of ninjas charging a defensive formation.

Depression works the same way: it depends on your silence. The only way depression can succeed is if you are a co-conspirator. If you turn on the lights, depression is powerless.

If you wait too long and your depression reaches a high level, it is much harder to ring the alarm bell when depression is in your bedroom, and it's got a knife to your throat. That is why we want to ring the bell as early as possible, and that is where we need our village.

My core tactic for dealing with depression is picking up the phone. I have a very simple rule: if I start to feel depressed, I tell the person closest to me.

If there is no one in the room, I call someone the second it starts to happen. Here's what I say: "I'm starting to feel depressed." Most people's response is, "Why are you telling me?" But here is the thing, I have turned on the lights and rung the bell; I've started the process of conquering depression.

Depression is like, "Uh-oh! What is happening? I don't like this; I don't know what to do in this situation." You have already done something very simple: you have killed the shame, you have removed a great deal of its power, and you have removed the secrecy.

Now someone knows what is happening – this will conquer a great deal of your depression.

If you suffer from a deeper depression that has been around for a longer period of time, this tactic alone won't help, but it buys you time.

It will buy you about one to two hours of grace depending on how your personality works to where you have to go for the second half of our village strategy.

The Depression Buster

I keep a list of things that I know I like to do. Before we continue this chapter, write down five to ten things that you know you like to do, but when you are depressed you don't like to do.

Some of the things that I enjoy are batting cages and driving ranges; pretty much anything with a range. Archery, definitely. Anything where you are hitting balls or throwing stuff at targets, I am into it on every level. Video games, yes. Movies, absolutely.

These are all things that I like to do; going to the gym, surfing, kayaking, paddle boarding. There are plenty of things that I like to do, but when I am depressed, I say to myself, "I don't want to do any of these things."

When my depression is really strong, I just like to lie in my bed. I don't even want to read a book or listen to music; I just lie there in a malaise. That is how powerful my depression gets – I just lie there unmoving on my bed. In that moment, I'll say, "I don't feel like…" and I'll name everything on my list. Depending on your situation, we are going to use the list in some different ways.

If you have a career or a particular reason you can't tell the nearest person, you can't involve everyone in your life because it will affect you. What you can do is designate a depression buddy, and you may even have five or ten.

These are people that you give your list to and you say, "If I call you and say I'm depressed, you need to come to me within the next ten minutes, and we need to do one of the things on this list. I'll pay for it."

Being a depression buddy is one of the best assignments a human can have. The job is to do something fun and awesome, for free. It's basically everyone's dream job.

"You mean if you have depression I have to go to the batting cages and have a couple of beers with you? I hope that you have depression forever; that sounds awesome!"

We are reversing a stigma. Now everyone wants to know the guy with depression. "I love going to the movies and now, whenever my friend is depressed, I get to go to the movies for free. Awesome!"

This technique will conquer your depression every time. As soon as you see the ninja across the moat, you throw up the old Bat Signal, put up a light in the sky, and ring the bell.

That depression is going to flee because we have conquered all the key ways that it's going to attack you: we have removed the secrecy, we have removed the shame, we have conquered loneliness, you are with another person, and you are doing something fun. You are doing something that takes up mental bandwidth.

The Power of Distraction

The reason depression gets you doing nothing is that if you are distracted, you forget that you are depressed. Have you ever had one of those moments where you go, "Oh, I forgot I was so depressed."

That's how you know it's just a thought. If you start doing something else, you will forget that you were "supposed" to be depressed, and the problem will disappear. Go to an interesting movie, and it will be hard to remember that you are depressed; it is too engaging.

Do not go to a depressing movie. For me, there are certain movies I cannot watch, certain books I cannot read, and I certainly can't listen to Radiohead when I'm feeling depressed; it only makes me more depressed.

There are certain types of music that activate or strengthen our emotions and our cycles, and I bet you have the music that you listen to when you're depressed.

Maybe your psychologist said you should listen to it to really experience the emotion, but what they are doing is enforcing the emotion and making the problem worse, not better.

If you listen to opposite music, it will put your mood in the opposite direction. If you listen to aggressive heavy metal when you are mad, you get madder. If you listen to it when you're happy, you still get a little bit mad. I know I do.

This is why we prepare our list in advance and give it to the person we've chosen. Now the power is in their hands. The more you can outsource the power, the easier it is to do.

Personally, I am now at a point where I give my list to people and say, "I'm feeling depressed, we have to do something right now." I will tell my wife and my kids.

My kids are so young they don't really understand, but if daddy says he's feeling depressed, they know it's time to do something fun, and there is a good chance of ice cream and a movie, or going swimming, or doing something awesome.

Just like reversing worrying (when I worry about something, and I know it is not going to happen), my kids know if daddy starts feeling depressed, it's time for a real fun day. I know the same thing – if I feel the first flicker of depression, I'm about to do something fun.

How strong do you think your depression will be at that point –

when your depression is a trigger sign that you are going to have a good day?

Say It out Loud

If you have a specific job where you can't do those things, you have to call your buddy. If you don't, then you just tell the person nearest to you, which is what I do. Yes, you can say this to a stranger. They won't understand.

"You know, I'm feeling depressed."

"Why are you telling me?"

But when you say it out loud, it beats the depression, and it gives you more time to go and find one of you depression buddies or someone to do stuff with.

It works really well if you are in a bar or restaurant and there's someone near you. You say, "Look, I'm feeling depressed. What I don't want to do is mingle, let's do something awesome. Can I buy you a bunch of drinks and we just talk about awesome stuff?" Nobody will say no to that!

This works on another level: you are now becoming a more fun, more awesome person that strangers will want to hang around. You are actually becoming a better person.

Depression can make you more popular when you add this simple approach to it. You don't have to pay for it, but it is a nice incentive that will make it a lot more likely that someone will help you.

If you are about to go to work, or you are at work, you are in a very limited environment, and you can't do much to alleviate that depression. First of all, I recommend you look at doing a half day and then go to do something fun.

If you look at statistics, many people in America take medical days off because they are too depressed to come into work.

If you say to your boss, "Look, sometimes I have bad depression, and when I do, it will make me stay home from work for two or three days. I am so depressed I can't leave the house. But if when it strikes I go to do something fun for one or two hours, it breaks the depression. So I'm going to miss a few hours of work, but I won't miss a few days."

Unless your boss is a total jerk, they are going to be understanding. What you are saying to your boss is sometimes you need to take a shorter break, so you don't have to take a longer break.

Your boss knows that if he gets a note from your shrink saying you can't come into work because you're too depressed, they're losing money – they're paying your bills while your desk is empty. It's much better for a company to let you take two hours off to fight your depression. This is why they let you take smoke breaks.

When you explain it as part of a medical problem and you say, "Look, I'm going to tell you and this is how I deal with it," then your boss should be accommodating. Most bosses will go, "I understand you have an emergency."

Do not abuse it or you will break it. Don't use it just because you want to go see a movie, or you don't feel like working that day, or you have a big project; that is not okay. This has to be used specifically for depression, or you will lose the effect.

You can set up a system where you always make up your missed hours by working overtime, when your mood is strong. As long as you are clear about the situation and not just trying to skip out on work, you can use this technique to stay on top of your depression.

When you use this technique, you crush your depression. The thought doesn't have time to get a beachhead, and it will disappear quickly.

Reflection Questions

1. Do you listen to music that matches your mood? Have you ever noticed that some music actually increases your mood?
2. What happens when you put on the music of a different emotion?
3. How does the thought of sharing your depression with

other people make you feel? Is it scary or can you focus on the light at the other side of the tunnel?
4. Which of these techniques gets you the most excited?

Activity

Your final activity for this chapter consists of writing five to ten go-to activities. You are also going to find a depression buddy or as many as you need.

Give them a copy of your list and say to them, "Sometimes I get depressed. When it starts happening, if I do something really fun, then the depression goes away. Here's twenty dollars in advance. When I call you, pick something from this list, come pick me up, and do it with me for two hours. You will save my life."

The reason I have five or ten people is that sometimes one of your buddies just can't do it. If you have a friend who is a surgeon busy operating on someone, you can't say, "Hey, stop that brain surgery and come to the batting cages!" But if you have five to ten people on the list and you give each one of them a call, someone will be available.

As you do this, you will get to the point where you can do this on your own. I love going to the batting cages, and I'll go to the batting cages by myself. One of the things I have been trying to find, because where I live it's so hard, is one of those machines you get to shoot the baseballs.

I would love to have that set up on the beach – hit baseballs into the ocean and have my dog fetch them for me. That's on my dream list; talk about a depression killer, that's awesome. My depression gave me that idea – my depression gives me a lot of good ideas for fun things to do.

When you give the list to a person for the first time, it might be a bit awkward, but once you have said it to one person, two through ten won't be a big deal. The secret is out; cat's out of the bag. In fact, if you want to do it to all of your friends at once, that is really easy too.

I recommend you keep a copy of the list in your wallet, so that no matter what, it's always there. Phone batteries dead? Still there. No signal or you can't get a line? Still there. I know we like to keep digital notes, but in this case, it's better to have something that works no matter what.

If you are feeling depressed and you can't call for help, that is when you need your list the most. Prepare your list, tell some people, and then join me in the next chapter.

Activity Two

Prepare a traveling distraction kit. Not every anti-depression activity has to be big. Any activity that requires all of your brainpower can shatter a depression cycle before it takes hold.

Sometimes I fire up a video game when I feel a flicker of depression. The games I play require so much focus that I don't have the mental bandwidth to be depressed at the same time.

The key with this type of activity is speed. Sometimes you just can't get away from work, or you're not near anything fun. You can't always leave the house. For these situations, you want to prepare some activities that you can do when you're alone or stuck somewhere.

I'm a big fan of adult coloring books and have an entire book on how powerful they are as a tool to fight depression. The secret to color books is their complexity. Each time you master a medium, you move on to a harder one.

When you are master of crayons, then you move on to colored pencils, then pastels and paints. You can keep the process infinitely complex, and this ensures that you never have mental space for depression.

Find some solo activities that you can do wherever you are. Stash some colored pencils and a coloring book on a desk at work, or toss a GameBoy in there. Keep some emergency supplies in the trunk of your car. All this preparation will make a big difference down the line.

10

ETERNAL VIGILANCE

When you implement the activities from the previous chapter, your life will change. These are very powerful tactics – practical and real-world solutions to a purely mental issue. Depression is a problem living in our imagination, in our minds.

You will begin to think that depression is gone forever, and I have gone through these phases as well. After a few months of doing this activity, no matter how strong your depression is, you will get to a point where your depression seems to be gone, and you feel cured.

You say to yourself, "I got over this depression, I never have to worry about it again." I want you to be careful because you will have relapses at certain points in your life. Preparing for failure is preparing to overcome that failure.

I developed my strategy twenty years ago. When I was seventeen, I decided to conquer depression on my own, and since then, I have never had to deal with a psychologist; I have never had to take another pill for my mind. Their solutions never worked for me; this is the only one that worked, and it changed my life.

That doesn't mean I don't experience depression. Just this past year, I had two or three instances where I felt depression coming on like a thundercloud, and that is why I recorded a podcast episode on depression.

I wanted to be sure that depression couldn't use shame against me. Depression was already whispering into my ear, "Your friends might understand what you deal with, but your audience will turn against you if they find out."

Rather than let that garbage thought gain a foothold, I shared my experience with the entire world on the most public forum I have access to. Needless to say, shame went scurrying back into the shadows.

Whether it's in ten or twenty years, any time you start to feel that flicker of depression, go back to your strategy, call a friend, or talk to the person nearest to you. Get it out in your voice as quickly as possible; say it out loud.

You can even shout in an empty room and shout it to your dog, "I'm starting to feel depressed," and you need to go to your battle stations, your depression emergency mode. Take the hammer and hit the glass.

Do not assume that, because depression hasn't hit you in a long time, it has lost its teeth. Depression has a secondary tactic, and this is the shame of becoming uncured. You go through the first few chapters, you conquer your depression, and you tell people, "Oh, I used to be depressed."

This is a phase I have been through myself; I would say, "I used to suffer from depression." By now, I realize that it is a lifelong struggle. It is not something I have every day, but it might be something I face once every year or every couple of years.

Once you have started telling people you're cured, it is hard to call someone up and say, "Hey, I'm suffering from depression," because they're going to say, "I thought you were cured?" That's our fear, right?

So don't go telling people that you are cured; it creates a problem down the line for you.

Don't Blink

It is important to prepare for the future and understand that sometimes our minds are very uncanny and can think of creative ways to bring the depression back.

You have to be eternally vigilant – you have to pay attention to when those moments happen to be able to say, "Something weird is going on."

It hadn't happened to me in such a long time, that when my depression came back the first time this year, I said, "What's going on? Why do I feel do feel so weird?" When I realized it was depression, I immediately called my father and said, "I'm depressed."

My father lives five thousand miles away, he's one of the people furthest away from me on the planet, but I had to say it to someone very quickly. I hadn't talked to my wife about my depression for some time because it hadn't come up in a while, so I called my dad first, and then I said to my wife, "We have got to do something really fun." She knows now, just like my kids do, that depression means it's going to be a really good day. Depression means daddy is not working.

Don't give yourself a secondary stigma and don't overstate the power of my solution. This way of dealing with depression is not permanent. It is very powerful, but it is not eternal.

You will occasionally suffer from flickers for the rest of your life when depression shows up, but as long as you use our strategy, the depression will disappear within an hour, and that is a wonderful feeling.

It is very empowering as long as you remember your strategy, so don't decide you're cured, throw away your card, and stop talking to all your friends.

Don't tell anyone that your depression is gone because you never know when it will come back. It might not be for fifty years, but you will be glad that you have that card when it does happen.

Reflection Questions

1. Have you thought about a life without depression?
2. Are you ready to be eternally vigilant?
3. How would it feel to think you are cured and discover your depression was sneaking back in? Would you feel shame and lose all your progress?
4. Are you glad that we have prepared for failure in advance?

Activity

Write down a promise to yourself: "I will not give my depression new powers. I will not decide and tell everyone that I am cured, so that I have to deal with the stigma of getting uncured.

I will not throw away my emergency plan. I will not forget this problem. Even if this comes back in fifty years, I'm going to be ready for it, because my strategy works."

11

THE EMERGENCY HAPPY LIST

I'm a guy of the eighties, which means I watched a lot of action movies. I watched all these movies where the hero has a big gun on his hip, and when that gun runs out of bullets, he grabs a small one off his ankle.

You don't see that much in movies now, but when I was a kid every hero had an ankle gun – it's your emergency get-out-of-jail card, the last-ditch effort, your "whatever I need to do to deal with the problem." That's what your list of happy things is.

Your list of things to do when you call your friend, the list of activities you love – that is your big gun. What we need to develop now is our ankle gun: a list of things in your life that you are grateful for.

Some families make you do this at Thanksgiving, so maybe you're groaning right now, but what I want you to do is take time to think about your accomplishments and your successes. Most of us haven't done this in a long time, and we forget so many things.

Having it handy, having a list you can pull out to read all of the best things you've done in life, is very effective. This is for when you can't reach anyone else or do any of those activities.

This is for when you are trapped in a snowstorm or locked in a house with no power, and there is no way to go outside. Talk about a dream scenario for your depression right, trapped with no power and it's getting cold outside.

I made one of these lists as part of an activity in my late twenties with someone who was going through an NLP course; it's very interesting. If you have a friend who is going through one of these courses, volunteer to be a guinea pig, I definitely recommend it.

He was essentially shrinking me. We would only do four or five sessions, but he would use really powerful techniques which still work for me ten years later. That is why NLP is a form of mental health than I'm a big fan of – it's effective, and it's built around big change quickly. He had me write down a list of all the things I accomplished in life; I came up with a list of about thirty-five things, most of which I had forgotten about.

When I was six years old, I won the Cub Scout race car tournament – also called the "Pinewood Derby." I beat children who were eighteen. Having a school trophy in my parents' house was one of my biggest achievements, and I forgot about it.

When I was in third grade, I won a math award and received a national medal for how I did on a math test. There are many other accomplishments, but not every one of them comes with a trophy. You can write down all of those great moments. For me, some of those moments are having my kids or teaching my daughter to swim.

We are now teaching my son to swim. We've been teaching him since he was about six weeks old, and now that he's about sixteen months, he's really jumped to the next level.

He's using floaties that are designed for a child that weighs about sixty percent more than him. He is swimming so well, that his swimming ability is beyond most of the things that are on the market. At sixteen months, he is swimming like a three-year-old, so all these tools are useless for us.

My daughter, who is such a good swimmer, hasn't used any kind of swimming help since she was three. In fact, she never even went through a floaties phase because she hated them, so she learned swimming a different way.

These are the things that I start to think about when I am feeling depressed. When I am locked in a situation where I can't use my primary strategy, this is my backup strategy. What are my greatest accomplishments in life, what are my achievements.

Bad Things Still Happen

We recently lost a child to a miscarriage. It's not the worst thing that can happen to a parent, but it is a pretty bad thing. My first thought was, let's spend more time with our other children and cling to the ones we have, and it helped us to overcome the risk of depression.

My wife, of course, was hit harder than I was because it was her body. She was far more upset, and she felt more to blame. Of course, we went through this experience together, and it is not her fault. It is very common for women who go through this to suffer from depression.

I said to her we should spend more time with the kids, and in fact, she is happier than she was two months ago because we're spending so much time with the children. She is the main engine beside my son jumping up in his swimming level.

It started with me teaching him first, but she has helped him accelerate to the point where now he can wear his high-level floaties and swim around the pool pretty effectively. You don't have to hold his hand; he can swim from one end to the other, that is his new accomplishment.

Spending time with the ones you love, spending time thinking about the ones you love, spending time thinking about your accomplishments will become a bulwark against depression when depression comes sneaking in.

Reflection Questions

1. Are there accomplishments in your life that you haven't thought about for a long time?

2. What does thinking about the bad moments in your life do to your emotional state?
3. Does thinking about my trauma put a tear in your eye?
4. What are some of your greatest accomplishments in life? Even if it takes an hour or a week to remember everything, create a list of all your achievements.

Activity

For your final activity, you're going to put together your ankle gun. Make a list of everything in life you are grateful for and everything in life you have accomplished – everything good you have ever done, every positive memory.

The list can be as long as you need; it can be ten things, or it can be a hundred. Work on it so it gets really big, print it out, and keep it with you all the time. You can have a version on your phone and a physical version as well.

You can laminate it – I am a big fan of laminating stuff, so it lasts forever.

This will prepare you for the future, and I worry that a lot of you won't do this activity. If you don't and you start to feel depressed, think about all of the things you have accomplished.

It's not my favorite as a final backup strategy – having an actual list is so much easier – but if you lose it, you can still sit down and think through it. If your list is long, it might take you ten minutes to read it; if you spend ten minutes reading about your accomplishments, it is hard to be depressed afterward. You'll be like. "Wow, I've done a lot of cool things I've forgotten about!"

12

THE FUTURE LOOKS SO BRIGHT I GOTTA WEAR SHADES

We're here, we're at the end of our journey, and I'm proud of you.

This book is about my own journey, from someone who first considered suicide when I was six years old to someone who has children and has totally taken dominion over my depression – someone who doesn't have to deal with it every day, but when that flicker comes up, I can deal with my problem quick enough to shut it down. I went from spending six weeks depressed to an hour or two, as long as I don't let depression catch me by surprise.

The ball is in your court now. I only have the ability to teach you how to deal with your depression; I can't make you do it. This is an active process; if you don't make your lists, do the activities, and you don't talk to people about your depression, then this book won't help you.

In a moment, you will be at the end of the book, and you can leave me a positive or a negative review. Before you leave a bad review, please do the activities. If you didn't do the activities or exercises, it's unfair to leave a review, and in fact, it's dishonest.

This is an instruction manual; if you don't follow the instructions, then you can't leave a review. If you do the activities and they don't work for you, email me. You have ways to contact me in the form at the back of the book – click that link and send me your email address; I will email you right away. I answer every email personally within twenty-four hours.

I can't be your depression buddy because I only check my email once a day, but I will help you develop a custom strategy to overcome what you are dealing with. This is a cooperative effort. I feel a sense of obligation to ensure that this path works for you.

If you are willing to put in the effort, I am willing to walk on the path with you to help you overcome your depression. We might have to develop a few unique techniques or creative strategies and that's okay; I'm willing to do it if you are. We are in this together – I have been where you are and I know it can be tough.

If this book helped you, if you went through the activities and they worked, I would love to hear about it. You can email me or leave a positive review; both are wonderful things. If you take pictures of yourself doing the activities from this book, like doing the mirror activity showing yourself depressed and then happy and how you had results, that would be awesome to see.

People would love that; it would be helpful and inspiring. Even a photo of you at the batting cages would be awesome to see. Just like I'm helping you, you can help the next person decide to grab this book when they see your smiling face.

This journey is about changing your life and transforming; helping you overcome something that can be a tough hurdle. I want you to have a big success. When you start to conquer your depression and have great experiences, I want to hear about it. Email me, tell me your stories, post it on social media and send me a link. That inspires me.

This is not a book about my own narcissism; it's a book about helping other people because someone asked for it. I suffered from depression for a very long time, but those days are behind me.

My life is amazing now; it turned a corner when I conquered

depression by turning from something that had control over me, to something that I have total dominion over. You can have the exact same thing; that's what I want for you.

MORE INFORMATION

Throughout this book I mentioned other books, images, links, and additional content. All of that can be found at:

https://servenomaster.com/depression

You don't have to worry about trying to remember any other links or the names of anything mentioned in this book. Just enjoy the journey and focus on taking control of your destiny.

LET'S SOAR TOGETHER

The hardest part of dealing with depression is going it alone. When you are in isolation, the night can seem so dark. Please join my FREE, private Facebook group filled with supportive people on the same path.

https://servenomaster.com/tribal

This is a great place to chat with me daily, share your experiences with the exercises and find a supportive group of people who are all on the same journey as you.

FOUND A TYPO?

While every effort goes into ensuring that this book is flawless, it is inevitable that a mistake or two will slip through the cracks.

If you find an error of any kind in this book, please let me know by visiting:

ServeNoMaster.com/typos

I appreciate you taking the time to notify me. This ensures that future readers never have to experience that awful typo. You are making the world a better place.

ABOUT THE AUTHOR

Born in Los Angeles, raised in Nashville, educated in London - Jonathan Green has spent years wandering the globe as his own boss - but it didn't come without a price. Like most people, he struggled through years of working in a vast, unfeeling bureaucracy.

And after the backstabbing and gossip of the university system threw him out of his job, he was "totally devastated" – stranded far away from home without a paycheck coming in. Despite having to hang on to survival with his fingernails, he didn't just survive, he thrived.

In fact, today he says that getting fired with no safety net was the best thing that ever happened to him – despite the stress, it gave him an opportunity to rebuild and redesign his life.

One year after being on the edge of financial ruin, Jonathan had replaced his job, working as a six-figure SEO consultant. But with his rolodex overflowing with local businesses and their demands getting higher and higher, he knew that he had to take his hands off the wheel.

That's one of the big takeaways from his experience. Lifestyle design can't just be about a job replacing income, because often, you're replicating the stress and misery that comes with that lifestyle too!

Thanks to smart planning and personal discipline, he started from scratch again – with a focus on repeatable, passive income that created lifestyle freedom.

He was more successful than he could have possibly expected. He traveled the world, helped friends and family, and moved to an island in the South Pacific.

Now, he's devoted himself to breaking down every hurdle entrepreneurs face at every stage of their development, from developing mental strength and resilience in the depths of depression and anxiety, to developing financial and business literacy, to building a concrete plan to escape the 9-to-5, all the way down to the nitty-gritty details of teaching what you need to build a business of your own.

In a digital world packed with "experts," there are few people with the experience to tell you how things really work, why they work, and what's actually working in the online business world right now.

Jonathan doesn't just have the experience, he has it in a variety of spaces. A best-selling author, a "Ghostwriter to the Gurus" who commands sky-high rates due to his ability to deliver captivating work in a hurry, and a video producer who helps small businesses share their skills with their communities.

He's also the founder of the Serve No Master podcast, a weekly show that's focused on financial independence, networking with the world's most influential people, writing epic stuff online, and traveling the world for cheap.

All together, it makes him one of the most captivating and accomplished people in the lifestyle design world, sharing the best of what he knows with total transparency, as part of a mission to free regular people from the 9-to-5 and live on their own terms.

Learn from his successes and failures and Serve No Master.

Find out more about Jonathan at:
ServeNoMaster.com

BOOKS BY JONATHAN GREEN

Non-Fiction

Serve No Master Series

Serve No Master

Breaking Orbit

20K a Day

Control Your Fate

Breakthrough (coming soon)

Habit of Success Series

PROCRASTINATION

Influence and Persuasion

Overcome Depression

Stop Worrying and Anxiety

Love Yourself

Conquer Stress

Law of Attraction

Mindfulness and Meditation Ultimate Guide

Meditation Techniques for Beginners

I'm Not Shy

Coloring Depression Away with Adult Coloring Books

Don't be Quiet

How to Make Anyone Like You

Develop Good Habits with S.J. Scott

How to Quit Your Smoking Habit

The Weight Loss Habit

Seven Secrets

Seven Networking Secrets for Jobseekers

Biographies

The Fate of my Father

Complex Adult Coloring Books

The Dinosaur Adult Coloring Book

The Dog Adult Coloring Book

The Celtic Adult Coloring Book

The Outer Space Adult Coloring Book

The 2nd Celtic Adult Coloring Book

Irreverent Coloring Books

Dragons Are Bastards

Fiction

Gunpowder and Magic

The Outlier (As Drake Blackstone)

ONE LAST THING

Reviews are the lifeblood of any book on Amazon and especially for the independent author. If you would click five stars on your Kindle device or visit this special link at your convenience, that will ensure that I can continue to produce more books. A quick rating or review helps me to support my family and I deeply appreciate it.

Without stars and reviews, you would never have found this book. Please take just thirty seconds of your time to support an independent author by leaving a rating.

Thank you so much!

To leave a review go to ->

https://servenomaster.com/depressionreview

Sincerely,
Jonathan Green
ServeNoMaster.com